NORTHERN ORACLE

D1248368

NORTHERN ORACLE

poems by Kirsten Dierking

Spout Press
Minneapolis, MN

Copyright © 2007 Kirsten Dierking

Kirsten Dierking
Northern Oracle
Poems

ISBN: 0-9659443-7-9

Cover Image: Jennifer Davis
Book Design: Chris Watercott
Cover Design: John Colburn

First Edition
Printed in the United States of America

Spout Press is a member of CLMP and is distributed
to the trade by Small Press Distribution, Berkeley CA
(www.spdbooks.org)

Published by Spout Press
PO Box 581067
Minneapolis, MN 55458-1067
(www.spoutpress.org)

ACKNOWLEDGEMENTS

The author would like to thank the following journals and anthologies, in which these poems previously appeared:

A View From the Loft: "At the Temperance River"

Comstock Review: "Daphne"

Great River Review: "Northern Oracle" and "Prayer"

Main Channel Voices: "Reading John Berryman" and "Refuge"

Out of Line: "For the Disappeared"

Poetry East: "Blue" and "The Migrations" and "Lucky"

Saunas: A Collection of Works Mostly in English by Finnish-Canadians, Finnish-Americans, and Finns: "Sauna on the Paurus Farm"

Sirius Verse: "Primitives"

Spout: "January 2003" and "Older Now"

The Talking Stick: "Moving, Part III"

To Sing Along the Way: Minnesota Women Poets from Pre-Territorial Days to the Present: "Northern Oracle"

Tomorrow, the River (a novel by Dianne Gray): "Point of Departure"

Water-Stone: "Moving, Part I" and "Border Lines" and "The Dangerous Body in January"

White Pelican Review: "The Ordinary"

Contents

AUTHOR'S NOTE

In the 1990's, two of my aunts went to Finland to meet my grandmother's family and discovered that many of her relatives were Sami. I tried to learn everything I could about the Sami culture, and I was particularly interested in traditional Sami animist beliefs. In many ways, these beliefs reflect my own sense that our lives are inextricably entwined with the spiritual in animals and nature.

The quotes introducing each section of poems are from *Trekways of the Wind* by Sami poet and artist Nils-Aslak Valkeapää, translated by Harald Gaski, Lars Nordström and Ralph Salisbury. American edition published by DAT in 1994. The poem "Sami With the Dog" is about a woodcut of the same name by Sami artist John Andreas Savio.

To learn more about the Sami, please visit my website: www.dierking.net

For my dad and mom,
Floyd and Nancy Paurus

THE ANIMIST

.

Life
writes in the air with a puff of breath
inscribes the water with a finger

Nils-Aslak Valkeapää
Trekways of the Wind

NORTHERN ORACLE

The aluminum prow scratches over
submerged vines, drifts through platters
of lily-pads. I lean to the side,
rest my hand on the water, touch
the sky of unknowable swimmers
feeding beneath me.

Sometimes I think the future begins
at the bottom of lakes. The next day rising
toward sound and action and easier
breathing. Darkness wanting
the candor of daylight, the simple shapes
of high noon, the plain faces with no
shadows.

I watch for an omen, but three feet
down, the sun disappears into murk
and secrets. The waves are reading
the lines of my palm, but show only this:
tomorrow coming like shimmering scales,
like transient bones fanned into dazzling,
silver fins.

BORDER LINES

Lying below the last open window
of late fall. Leaves drifting against
the screen like papery moths. The dog

with a long, groaning exhale, releases
herself from vigilance. Patrick turns over,
laughs out loud again in his dream.

How much will I miss, closing my eyes?
In the dark, my body, laid out for sleeping,
looks insubstantial as chimney smoke.

Now, no alarm, just a sudden waking
in colder weather, the future already underway.
My back cradled, my dark hair dusted with snow.

BLUE

Often,
in November.

Thinking about
irretrievable things:

the scarlet leaves,
the old houses,

the good and bad
invisible dead.

Out in the yard,
the thickening sky

settles into
the empty trees.

Only the cloth
of your blue robe

keeps you from drifting
apart in the gray.

Only the blue
cloth of your robe

keeps you from being
quite unseen.

Despite the clatter
of someone you love

making tea
in the other room,

you can't stop
the snow from coming

you can't stop
yourself becoming

all the white,
expressionless snow.

READING JOHN BERRYMAN

Berryman committed suicide in Minneapolis

Yesterday,
while reading a poem
called *He Resigns*,
the winter sky
caught me off-guard
with a bright unbroken
aquamarine, a vast sweep
of Caribbean sea,
in January, in Minnesota.

For a long time
I floated between
the page and the view,
the two exquisite
expressions of blueness.
After awhile,
I closed the book.
But the glorious sky,
I thought I could never
willingly leave.

SHOVELING SNOW

If day after day I was caught inside
this muffle and hush

I would notice how birches
move with a lovely hum of spirits,

how falling snow is a privacy
warm as the space for sleeping,

how radiant snow is a dream
like leaving behind the body

and rising into that luminous place
where sometimes you meet

the people you've lost. How
silver branches scrawl their names

in tangled script against the white.
How the curves and cheekbones

of all my loved ones appear
in the polished marble of drifts.

THE ANIMIST

*"In the beginning of things, men were animals
and animals were men."*
—*from an Algonquin tale*

In April when
the ground inhales
the yellow sun
and the grass
is suddenly
sweet and green
and you find yourself
lying down
and rolling in it,
you admit an animal
lives inside you.

If that kind
of exuberant creature
exists within
your plain skin,
what is hiding
inside the tree,
what kind
of glorious spirit
lives inside
the wildflower?

SAILING ON LAKE SUPERIOR

Before us now the edge of the earth,
below us the nearly endless cold.
Around us nothing but shimmering
water,
the miles of empty and sparkling blue.

For a few hours, the sail fills on
toward infinity. Shadows of
our delicate bodies ebb and flow
across the deck of our delicate boat.

What if the beautiful days, the good
and pacific temperate moments,
weren't just lovely, but everything?
What if I could let it fall away
in the wake, that ache to extract
meaning from vastness?

Let this suffice; the ease of thinking
it all goes on, whether we're here
to see it or not. The splashing waves,
the suntipped gulls arcing across
the radiant world.

DAPHNE

*To escape the sun god Apollo, Daphne asked
to be turned into a tree.*

Some people said
it was giving in.

The way I relaxed
my back in the dirt,

seeded my scalp
with tangles of leaves,

let my eyes grow
hard and crazy

as knots, arms shielding
the body like bark.

Giving in,
the way I allowed

my mouth to dissolve
in a budding relief

of lush and blossom,
twig and garden,

where pleas became
branches, fear

became forest,
and sleep like a veil

of camouflage green,
stilling the heart,

defying even
the furious Sun.

JULY IN THE GARDEN

The sky relaxes its thick belly,
a muggy bulge of orange heat
hanging over the belt of horizon.
Muscles relax to the edge of melting,
ease the chalky friction of bones.

Humidity like a warm hand
kneading the clench of your
curved back. You stop leaning
into the future. You find the pause
between the green and sultry moments.

When you are still, tomato vines
wind a bloom of yellow stars
around your waistline. Air
like a lush bouquet for breathing.
All the birds of paradise singing.

THE ORDINARY

It's summer, so
the pink gingham shorts,
the red mower, the neat rows
of clean smelling grass
unspooling behind
the sweeping blades.

A dragonfly, black body
big as a finger, will not leave
the mower alone,
loving the sparkle
of scarlet metal,
seeing in even a rusting paint
the shade of a flower.

But I wave him off,
conscious he is
wasting his time,
conscious I am
filling my time
with such small details,
distracting colors,

like pink checks,
like this, then that,
like a dragonfly wing
in the sun reflecting
the color of opals,
like all the hours
we leave behind,
so ordinary,
but not unloved.

PRAYER

Common sparrows
flit from the green
bouquets of branches
onto the grass,
onto the feeder—

like happiness
to be winged
and delicate
and adept enough
to land everywhere
on this earth,
lightly.

THE FRAGILE ORGANICS

It is not until later that I realize
that the summer has passed

And when did that happen?

Nils-Aslak Valkeapää
Trekways of the Wind

POINT OF DEPARTURE
for girls at 14

A gull circles
and splashes down
and paddles into
a perfect circle
of sudden sun,
gray wings
lighted into
a radiant silver,
body a white
splendor of feathers,
the rise and fall
of waves against
the heart of the bird
as graceful as clouds.

It makes me think,
maybe a place
is waiting for us
where we leave behind
our clumsy feet,
our everyday clothing,
and swim for the spotlight,
our own shining time
on the water.

RAINSTORM

I used to be able
to dive backwards
into the pool,
spine curved, legs taut,
hands reaching
blindly behind me
to cleave the water.

It seems I slowed
into older limbs
as naturally
as rain running down
the face of the window.
On what day
could I no longer
perform that dive?

Sometimes
I dream about it.
No fatigue
or hesitation.
Body arched
with effortless grace,
poised over
the waiting blue.

IN SEPTEMBER

A manic gabble
from hidden grackles
concealed high
in the old oaks,
visible only
the tip of a feather,
ebony belly,
a graphite claw
sidling up
a leafy branch.

All at once
they fall silent,
all together
they rise up,
the rush of air
under thousands of wings
like a great exhale,
blue sky blotted out
by the dark cloak
of the flock
as it ripples
and veers south,

the mum oaks,
limbs raised
as if they'd flung
the noise skyward,

as if they were
complicit in
their own green leaved ending,
as if they had
accepted the loss
of the migrating birds,
while it feels to me
a little like grief,
another summer
flying away.

OLDER NOW

Bent down to unbraid
my sandal straps,
the skin of my hands

plump and smooth
in heat as close as bandages.
I didn't see

the evening coming,
I didn't notice
the last hot spell,

I was listening to
a remake of a song
I loved at twenty-one,

for a moment I felt
a terrible craving for all
the things I wanted then,

it felt like a clock
was leaping from summer
to longing to aging,

how did I get here

holding my sandals,
walking barefoot
over the snow.

THE DANGEROUS BODY
IN JANUARY

My knee on its way
to wreckage now

and at night waking up
to the little drama

of the cold hour
when unmaintainable joints

will falter,
and falling behind,

and falling still,
under white sheets

like snow that quiets
the birds in winter,

I'll have to let
the world go,

I'll have to watch it
walking away.

IN THE PRODUCE AISLE

In the vivid red
of the fresh berries,
in the pebbled skin
of an emerald lime,
in the bright colors
of things made
to be transitory,

you see the same
loveliness
you find in your own
delicate flesh,
the lines fanned
around your eyes
charming like
the burnish
of plums,

your life like
all the other
fragile organics,
your soft hand
hovering over
the succulent apple,
you reach for it,
already transforming.

EXAMINED LIFE WITH WILDERNESS

from the painting "Examined Life with Ric-Rac"
by Deborah Padgett

Sky tinted
the pale purple
of early twilight,
upcoming sleep.

Gray mountains
living the span
of geology.

Linen clouds,
the first suggestion
of evening stars.

Black shadows
sliding like lashes
over the colored eye
of the lake.

She leaves behind
a strand of hair.
Presses a fingerprint
into the dirt.

Accepts a heart
built like other
warm-blooded things:
brief, and gritty,
and passionate.

But sometimes aching
for mountain or star.
A way to latch on
to permanence.

ABANDONED BARN

Emptiness has filled the walls
with the wistful quiet of still water.
As if what's been abandoned here
is the ordinariness of anyone's life,
the common tasks and heavy lifting,
the animal sighs and everyday talk,
the oats running like sand or time
to fill and refill the empty containers.

Now just traces of grain and straw,
the damp smell of earth and leather.
Trickles of light stirring the gray,
insensible dust. Over and over,
things we hope we will always have
are lost, or ending. And yet, this rest
after long work. This falling apart
to the grace of birdsong.

UNSTABLE

As time passed
the Uldas had enough
and traded the evil ones
out of their own world

That is how the earth got them
and the very worst ones
began to rule as rulers and superiors
some dressed in uniforms
and gave themselves positions

And people received
a road of suffering
on which to compete

Nils-Aslak Valkeapää
Trekways of the Wind

FOR THE DISAPPEARED

At recess once I was playing tag,
running away from the other kids,
when I opened my eyes, I was
lying face down in a far corner
of the empty schoolyard, I never
really knew what happened.

How easily the continuous thread
of our lives can be broken. The
missing pieces we never get back.
The dark spells we wear like a veil
to our last moment, not knowing,
not ever understood.

9/11

She drives
to the airport

and even before
they stop her car

and even before
they ask which flight

her husband was on,
she feels the weight

of her heart falling
story by story

through atriums
of throat and chest,

collapsing like
a stricken building,

like stars at the end
of a universe.

9/12 IN THE MIDWEST

Everything seems alien
except the birds.

Brown feathers,
straw-colored beaks,

more cackle and vigor
than singing or grace,

offering us
a flock to build

a familiar scene,
lending us

the common grit
of durable wings.

A DREAM OF A DIFFERENT ENDING

A plane is crashing,
not in fire, or sudden

spirals, but coming
down so slow,

I could almost
save it,

simple as catching
snow in my hand.

Falling, it makes
a whistling sound,

faint like the gasp
of a parting cloud.

As if the heavens
were carved in two,

as if the world
ran out of air.

When I look again,
the passengers

are walking safely
out of the wreck,

their eyes untroubled,
their hearts intact.

As if those moments
of almost dying

weren't a torment,
like none of this

had happened at all.

ORANGE ALERT

Today the sparrows are wheeling about,
starving after too many days
of sub-zero weather.

I go outside to fill the feeder.
I feel uneasy. The fate of all this
delicate life in the air above us.

Great oaks push their limbs
through gray sky. I raise my arms
high like branches, press against
the threat of storms.

A bird flies toward the window glass,
but turns aside at the last moment.

JANUARY 2003

Every night a lethal story
about the ice. Slick, unstable,
the lakes forming open holes
of black water, cold liquid
shaded the color of winter night.

So many are rushing toward it.
Always amazed when the landscape
wavers, always surprised
when the frigid water won't let go.

Tonight, on tv, the president
tells us the state of the union.
Words in the language
of freezing lakes, threats
with the footing of shifting snow.

So many cheering for war.
Applause like the crack
of rotten ice under our feet.

HOUSE WITH A YELLOW
RIBBON AROUND A TREE

Sometimes when she's
slicing a lemon,
or measuring butter,
or ridding the garden
of dandelions,
she finds herself
holding her breath.

She can't believe
how constrictive
that cheerful circle
of yellow ribbon.
Like the petaled fringe
of a sunflower,
enclosing the seeds
of fear in her heart.

APRIL

As migrating birds
appear like clouds

of bright confetti,
as the sun covers

our bodies with warmth,
as even the earth

insists we turn
from shadow

into a season
of light,

a local kid
reported among

the dead
this morning,

April, the war
escalating.

THE PATH HOMEWARD

My home is in my heart
it migrates with me

> *Nils-Aslak Valkeapää*
> *Trekways of the Wind*

SAMI WITH THE DOG

a color woodcut by John Andreas Savio

I.

In rolling waves
of lavender tundra

the Sami walker
strides ahead,

his good dog
held to his side

by the great weight
of a dog's heart,

they lean
forward,

the path
is homeward,

even the cold
of the north sky

is an old friend,
companionable.

II.

An ocean of snow
cascades through

the midwest woods,
the gray sky

expansive like
a dream

or tundra,
as we turn

for home
the good dog

strays then walks
again at my side,

in any land
a dog's love

is deep and easy,
companionable.

ME AND MY PARROTS

a painting by Frida Kahlo

Abandoned parrots
will pluck their feathers
and shred their skin
to show the word lonesome.

In Frida's painting,
her birds are brilliantly
plumed in her arms,
as yet unaware that parrots
live as long as people,
sometimes longer.

She saves on canvas
the things she can:
the green wings and
yellow hoods, the plush
breasts in powder blue.

But paints her eyes
not meeting the eyes
of the parrots. Draws
her arms like a cross
to cover the cheerful birds.
Her own bones their cage
and cradle and amulet.

PRIMITIVES

At the foot of the bed,
the dog is dreaming.

Runners calling
from deep inside

the massed trees,
elliptical noses

rising toward
the eye of the moon.

He lifts his throat
from the patterned quilt,

howls a slow atonal cry;
a silver blade

sliding the scale
of violin strings.

I snap awake
in the hunting dark,

slick with sweat,
all the fur

at the back of my neck
instinctively rising.

LIVING WITH ANIMALS

"silence is so accurate" —*Mark Rothko*

Every evening
you sit close,
bodies pressed
against each other.

Every night
your sleeping spines
spiral like
the Milky Way
beside each other.

You leave no spaces.
You leave no room
for misunderstanding.

How easy it is
to live in peace
with animals.

How accurately
love can be conveyed
in silence.

THE MIGRATIONS

The last of the geese are out on the lake
in a final circle of open water,
wings folded close to the body,
white breasts bared to the cold.

Beautiful how the sharp black
of the birds' necks arches against
the silver light, sways over
the sheer veneer of glinting ice.

The snow begins, a little, softly,
like a slanting veil falling between
your hands and the birds. You try
to keep what you love close, and yet
you love things that can't help leaving.

The geese are slipping farther from land,
receding into the thickening whiteness.
How distant they are already from home.
How far they are going away from you now.

THE OPERA AFTER
FLURRY DIED

You can't understand harmony now.
You can't stand loveliness.
Even the most beautiful music
passes you by like a bored ghost.

You are more in tune with the scrape
of chairs in the audience. The rasping cough
that ripples throughout the dark house
and won't stop.

On stage, the tenor is losing the girl
he adores. You reach for the hand
of your partner beside you, tonight
everyone dying of love.

GRAVITY

When things really
leave you
for good,
again this year
an old dog,
something thins
inside the body.
Now sometimes
while standing
in line,
or waiting
in traffic,
I feel my hands
begin to rise.
One day
I will lose
so much
I will weigh
no more
than a ray
of light,
and drift up,
a small shining,
the bright remainder
of things
I loved.

MOVING

I.

We paint the exterior
white, the foundation

white, the windowsills
white, the porch,

the railings, garage door
white, we move the

geraniums, red,
out front,

we do all this
to sell the house,

or maybe to make it
not our house,

shrouding a friend,
pulling the paint

over the walls
like a white sheet.

II.

Nothing here
feels like home.
My limbs bruised
from bumping up
against the jut
of angled hallways,
the unexpected
frames of doors.

All day long
shadows of trees
ripple against
the window glass.
Until the walls,
even my heart
is wavering.

I can't be still.
I can't quite
extract myself
from the old house.

The fingerprints
I left on doorways.
The flowerbeds
I planted so
revealingly
all the private shades
of my self.

III.

Alone inside
the redwood skin
of this new house,
I spell my name,

each syllable
echoing off
the empty walls
like conversation,

each character
moving into
a vacant room
like furniture,

for the first time,
the air of this place
leans against me
like a comfort.

Out in the yard,
the rings inside
the scarlet oak
begin recording.

IV.

Snow over
the silver birches

snow inside
the floating arms

of blue spruce,
night coming down

like a black cat
to curl against

the evergreens,
right now

the heart of this land
coursing through me,

taste of maple
red of oak

body casting down
its roots.

MY HUSBAND DRIVES ME
TO URGENT CARE

Our car rolls
on the quiet street
like a small wave
through the empty ocean,

falling snow
like a silent shower
of meteor stars,

the midnight faces
of glass buildings
heavy with sleep,
or loneliness.

Even inside
the raging grippe
of ache and fever
I know you're beside me.

I rest my forehead
against my hands.
You dressed me,
you remembered
my mittens.

SLEEP TIGHT

At the end of an illness
I wake up coughing,
to wind shuffling

over the roof,
a scatter of rain
on skylight glass.

A sudden noise
is only the furnace
coming on,

heating the air
to just the safe degree
of darkness.

I lay there, healing,
not scared, unstartled,
shadows quiet

against the walls,
closets hiding
nothing but clothes.

The hardest hours
of mending
over,

stitches closing
slits in the bedsheets,
wounds in the body,

gaps in the skin,
the nighttime,
sleep.

Crucial, like love,
this sense of soundness,
sensuous ease.

This resting
inside an altered life,
comfortable.

A PICTURE IN OUR STYLE

Blaues Pferd I, a painting by Franz Marc

A blue horse.
Neck bent

to bow the head.
To half-close

the eyes in peace.
To show a chest

of good heart,
kind color,

coat the hue
of small mercies,

bright music,
deep rest.

These are things
I would say

about our home.
As if we had

around our walls,
those gold meadows,

blue horses,
that warm

and constant
cherry sky.

REFUGE

Awake late. Daylight draped
over the bed in a lazy expanse
of orange time. Through the doorway
the day spreads out in loping waves,
like an empty body of summer water,
aquamarine. No obligations
but feeding the dogs. Later,
a little time in the garden.

When your husband gets home,
you eat, wash dishes, and sometimes
while talking, often in passing,
you catch hands, the small assurance
I'm here, I'm here. Happiness feeling
light and simple as yellow balloons,
why sometimes does it seem so hard
to get to this, to live in this: the shine
of air in contented houses.

SAUNA ON THE PAURUS FARM

"koti" Finnish for "home

My parents used a battered dipper
to ladle water over the fieldstones,
the round rocks like gray whales
spouting hot geysers of steam.

My sister and I sweated until
it seemed our bones grew malleable,
until we could no longer breathe
in air the thickness of liquid sun

and rushed for the cool of the
north-starred sky, our bodies
washed in permanent warmth: clean,
with family, and koti, belonging.

LUCKY

All this time,
the life you were
supposed to live
has been rising around you
like the walls of a house
designed with warm
harmonious lines.

As if you had actually
planned it that way.

As if you had
stacked up bricks
at random,
and built by mistake
a lucky star.

SPECIAL THANKS

My heartfelt gratitude and love to my husband and first reader, Patrick Dierking, and to all the other friends, family, readers, and fellow writers who are so generous with their time, their talents and their encouragement: Dianne Gray, Kay Korsgaard, Deborah Keenan, Nancy Paurus, Floyd Paurus, Robin Paurus, Leslie Rentmeester, Ann Schroder, Talia Nadir, Claire Kirch, and the writing group - Teresa Boyer, Carol Pearce Bjorlie, Ann Iverson, Janet Jerve, Marie Rickmyer, Kathy Weihe and Liz Weir. Thanks to John Colburn and everyone at Spout Press, and special thanks to Michelle Filkins, gifted reader, writer, editor, and good friend. I am very grateful to the Minnesota State Arts Board, the Loft Literary Center, and SASE /Intermedia Arts/The Jerome Foundation for generous grants that helped support my work as a poet. And I will always be grateful to the Graduate Liberal Studies program at Hamline University for helping me find my voice as a writer.

ABOUT THE AUTHOR

Kirsten Dierking is the author of *One Red Eye*, a book of poems, and her writing has appeared in numerous journals and anthologies, including *Water-Stone*, *Poetry East*, and *To Sing Along the Way: Minnesota Women Poets from Pre-Territorial Days to the Present*. She is the recipient of a Minnesota State Arts Board Grant for literature, a Loft Literary Center Career Initiative Grant, and a SASE/Jerome Grant. Kirsten received a bachelor's degree in international affairs and history from the University of Colorado, and a master's degree in creative writing from Hamline University. She teaches humanities courses at Anoka-Ramsey Community College, and lives with her husband Patrick in Arden Hills, Minnesota.